THE ULTIMATE
BOOK OF
KID CONCOCTIONS 2

More Than 65 New Wacky, Wild & Crazy Concoctions

John E. Thomas
Danita Thomas

A Publication of The Kid Concoctions Company

CREDITS:

Cover art design:	Robb Durr
Computer art & graphics:	Christopher Roberto
Cover photography:	Jack Dragga
Illustrations:	Robb Durr, Zachariah Durr
Copy editing:	Margaret Briller

The Kid Concoctions Company
14761 Pearl Road, PMB #161
Strongsville, OH 44136 USA

ISBN: 0-9661088-1-7

Manufactured in the United States of America
10 9 8 7 6 5 4 3 2 1

Visit our website: www.kidconcoctions.com
Email: KidConcoct@aol.com

Notice: The information in this book is true, complete, and accurate to the best of our knowledge. All suggestions and recommendations are made without guarantees on the part of the authors or the publisher. The author and publisher disclaim all liability incurred in connection with the use of this information.

Dedication

To all of you who supported and believed in Kid Concoctions and made it a success with us, we dedicate this book to you.

Acknowledgments

We would like to thank the following people, whose valuable contributions made this book possible:

Robb Durr
Zachariah Durr
Christopher Roberto
Margaret Briller

We would also like to personally thank others who helped us in our journey to make Kid Concoctions all it is today:

Daniel J. Levin
Our friends at Fitness Quest
Wallace D. Gilbert
Grover & Gloria Thomas
Sandra K. Shaft
Our children:
Kyle, Kalie and Kellen

Foreword

Just like our first best-selling book, The Ultimate Book of Kid Concoctions, these recipes are designed to create commercial quality projects quickly, easily and inexpensively by using nothing more than common household ingredients. Many of these recipes are our own original creations and some are classics that we have updated for families of today. We believe this book will be a great resource for children, parents, teachers, grandparents, day-care providers, and anyone wanting to put a smile on a child's face. We hope these concoctions will bring your family as much enjoyment as they have ours.

Kid Concoctions have become a well respected favorite among the educational community. These easy-to-do recipes combine math, science, reading, arts, and crafts as well as life skills such as measuring, into hours of fun.

We encourage you to create Kid Concoctions with a child in your life. It is a wonderful way to spend quality time together and build everlasting memories. Kid Concoctions have been designed to assist in building a child's confidence and self-esteem by encouraging in them the desire to explore, create, learn, and experiment.

Because children have so much potential, we encourage you to foster creativity within them by sharing ideas and encouraging them to explore their own creative ideas.

Happy Concocting!!

John & Danita Thomas

CONTENTS

 *Adult supervision is recommended for all projects and recipies.*

SPLONGEE FLYER

This flying starburst shaped ball is fun to play with indoors or out.

WHAT YOU WILL NEED:

3 small sponges (use different colored sponges)
1 plastic cable tie
1 large rubber band
Scissors

HOW TO CONCOCT IT:

1. Cut each sponge into thirds lengthwise.
2. Stack the cut sponges on top of each other in three rows of three.
3. Grab the stack of sponges in the center and twist the stack once.
4. Place plastic cable tie through the center of the rubber band.
5. Secure a plastic cable tie around the center of the twisted stack, pulling it as tightly as possible.
6. Trim the plastic cable tie down as close to the eye as possible.
7. Put the rubber band on the tip of your thumb, pull back the sponge ball, and release to shoot.

CONCOCTION TIPS & IDEAS:

◆ Use nylon sponges. They stay soft, cost less, and come in a wide variety of colors.
◆ Set up targets made of decorated toilet paper tubes and try to knock them over with your Splongee Flyers.

SURPRISE SOAPS

Ball shaped soaps that reveal secret treasures as kids wash.

WHAT YOU WILL NEED:

1 cup grated Ivory® soap
1/4 cup warm water
Food coloring
Small rubber animals or toys

HOW TO CONCOCT IT:

1. Mix water, soap, and food coloring together in a medium bowl. Stir the mixture until it begins to stiffen.
2. Remove the mixture from the bowl and knead it until it is the consistency of a very thick dough.
3. Roll the dough into the shape of a ball.
4. Make a hole in the center of the ball big enough to hide treasures in.
5. Fill the hole with treasures and seal with some extra dough.
6. Allow Surprise Soaps to dry overnight before using.

CONCOCTION TIPS & IDEAS:

♦ Mold the Surprise Soap dough into different shapes and sizes.
♦ Add a few drops of perfume or cologne to make scented Surprise Soaps.

SNOWY FOAM PAINT

Snowy Foam Paint looks like real snow and dries to a plastic foam-like finish.

WHAT YOU WILL NEED:

1 cup white school glue
1 cup white shaving cream

HOW TO CONCOCT IT:

1. Mix shaving cream and glue together in a small bowl.
2. Let the mixture set for 2 minutes.
3. Use a brush to paint with Snowy Foam Paint.

CONCOCTION TIPS & IDEAS:

♦ Add a few drops of food coloring to Snowy Foam Paint and create colorful pictures.
♦ Dip foam balls into Snowy Foam Paint to create snowmen and other snow-like sculptures.

MAGIC CANDLE ART

Layers of colored wax create this unique and unusual candle.

WHAT YOU WILL NEED:

Pieces of old used candles separated by color
Kitchen grater
Candle wick
Baby food jar (with the label removed)

HOW TO CONCOCT IT:

1. Have an adult grate the candle pieces into a fine powder.
2. Layer different colors of the candle powder in a baby food jar.
3. Gently push a candle wick into the center of the jar.

CONCOCTION TIPS & IDEAS:

♦ Try making Magic Candles in different types of glass containers like jelly and pickle jars.
♦ Decorate the outside of your Magic Candle with colorful stickers to create a wonderful gift for any holiday.
♦ Magic Candles should be lit and supervised by an adult.

MARBLE PAINT

You'll have fun while painting amazing works of art with marbles.

WHAT YOU WILL NEED

Marbles
2 Tbs. liquid tempera paint
Plastic cup
Large shallow pan or pie tin
Paper

HOW TO CONCOCT IT:

1. Pour tempera paint into the plastic cup.
2. Gently drop 3-4 marbles into the paint.
3. Place a sheet of paper inside the pan so it is laying flat on the bottom.
4. Spoon out the paint covered marbles from the plastic cup and into the pan.
5. Tilt the pan side to side to create your Marble Paint design. Let the paint dry before handling the paper.

CONCOCTION TIPS & IDEAS:

◆ Use Marble Paint to create greeting cards, wrapping paper, party invitations, and stationery.
◆ Try using different colors of paint on the same sheet of paper to create interesting designs.

SPRAY GLUE

A great easy way to make your own spray adhesive & shellac.

WHAT YOU WILL NEED:

3/4 cup water
1/4 cup white school glue
Spray bottle

HOW TO CONCOCT IT:

1. Mix glue and water together in a small bowl until blended.
2. Pour the mixture into the spray bottle.
3. Shake the mixture well before each use.

CONCOCTION TIPS & IDEAS:

◆ Add a few drops of food coloring to create colored Spray Glue.
◆ Use Spray Glue to put a shiny finish on dried clay sculptures or to stick large pieces of paper together.

BATH & BODY PAINT

With this wild concoction you can paint your body and get clean at the same time.

WHAT YOU WILL NEED:

1/4 cup liquid baby bath
1 Tbs. cornstarch
2-3 drops food coloring
Plastic ice cube tray

HOW TO CONCOCT IT:

1. Mix liquid baby bath and cornstarch together until blended.
2. Add 2-3 drops of food coloring.
3. Pour the mixture into a plastic ice cube tray and paint.

CONCOCTION TIPS & IDEAS:

◆ Use a paint brush to paint your body and the side of the bath tub.
◆ Bath & Body Paint also makes a great finger paint when used on wax paper.

STICKY BREAD DOUGH

A wonderful dough kids can use to create ornaments, beads and sculptures.

WHAT YOU WILL NEED:

4 slices of white bread (with the crusts cut off)
4 Tbs. of white school glue
4-6 drops food coloring

HOW TO CONCOCT IT:

1. Break the bread into small pieces and place in a bowl.
2. Add white school glue and food coloring.
3. Stir until blended together.
4. Knead the mixture with your hands until it forms a soft dough.
5. Sculpt with the Sticky Bread Dough and allow it to dry overnight until hard.

CONCOCTION TIPS & IDEAS:

♦ Roll the Sticky Bread Dough out on wax paper and cut different shapes with cookie cutters to make ornaments and gift tags.
♦ Use 1 Tbs. of coffee instead of food coloring to give Sticky Bread Dough an antique-like finish.

SILLY STAINED GLASS

With this amazing concoction, you can create the look of real stained glass with household items.

WHAT YOU WILL NEED:

Colored tissue paper
Liquid starch
Paint brush

HOW TO CONCOCT IT:

1. Cut colored tissue paper into different shapes and sizes.
2. Paint the liquid starch on a clear plastic or glass surface.
3. Place the tissue paper pieces on top of the starch covered item while smoothing out any wrinkles and covering all blank spaces.
4. Silly Stained Glass will dry in 4-6 hours.

CONCOCTION TIPS & IDEAS:

◆ Create a sparkling candle by covering the outside of a baby food jar with Silly Stained Glass and then placing a small votive candle inside the jar.
◆ After your Silly Stained Glass has dried, you can create the look of lead by outlining the tissue paper pieces with a black felt tip marker.

MAGIC FLOWER TRANSFERS

Transfer the image and color of real flowers onto tee shirts.

WHAT YOU WILL NEED:

Fresh flowers (impatiens, geraniums & pansies work best)
Rubber mallet
Clear plastic wrap
100% cotton tee shirt

HOW TO CONCOCT IT:

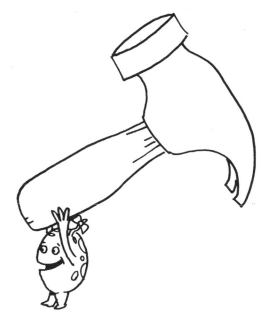

1. Place flowers in an interesting pattern face down on the cotton fabric.
2. Cover the flower design with a layer of clear plastic wrap.
3. Gently hit the flowers with the rubber mallet, being careful not to miss any parts of the flowers.
4. Remove the plastic wrap and flowers from the fabric to reveal your Magic Flower Transfer.

CONCOCTION TIPS & IDEAS:

♦ Try Magic Flower Transfers on paper and envelopes to create custom stationery.
♦ Use Magic Flower Transfers on cloth napkins and pillow cases.

FRUITY TIE-DYE SHIRTS

Create cool temporary tie-dye tee shirts using nothing more than fruit flavored drink mix.

WHAT YOU WILL NEED:

1 package of unsweetened drink mix (2 Tbs.)
1/4 cup white vinegar
2 cups cold water
Rubber bands
Tee shirt
Rubber gloves

HOW TO CONCOCT IT:

1. Mix drink mix, vinegar, and water together in a small pot.
2. Bring the mixture to a boil over medium heat.
3. Remove the mixture from heat and let it cool.
4. Scrunch the tee shirt up into a ball and wrap several rubber bands around it.
5. Put on rubber gloves and dip the tee shirt in the Fruity Tie-Dye solution several times.
6. Allow the tee shirt to sit overnight until dry, then remove the rubber bands to reveal your Fruity Tie-Dye shirt.

CONCOCTION TIPS & IDEAS:

◆ Use Fruity Tie-Dye to color Easter Eggs.
◆ Make several different colors of Fruity Tie-Dye to create multicolored shirts.

FREEZE POP PAINT

Budding young artists will enjoy painting with these frozen paint pops.

WHAT YOU WILL NEED:

2 Tsp. powdered tempera paint
1/3 cup water
Wax coated paper cup
Craft stick
Plastic wrap

HOW TO CONCOCT IT:

1. Mix powder tempera paint and water together.
2. Pour the mixture into a wax coated paper cup.
3. Cover the cup with plastic wrap, then insert a craft stick through the plastic wrap into the center of the cup.
4. Place the cup in the freezer and freeze until solid.
5. Remove the paper cup and plastic wrap from the Freeze Pop Paint.
6. Dip the Freeze Pop Paint into water and paint on white paper.

CONCOCTION TIPS & IDEAS:

♦ Make Freeze Pop Paint in a plastic ice cube tray instead of a wax paper cup.
♦ Use Freeze Pop Paint to create cool wrapping paper and greeting cards.

APPLE HEAD PEOPLE

Kids of all ages will be amazed watching big apples turn into delightful little Apple Heads.

WHAT YOU WILL NEED:
1 red delicious apple
1 cup lemon juice
1/4 cup table salt

HOW TO CONCOCT IT:
1. Have an adult peel the apple.
2. Draw a face on the apple using a toothpick.
3. Have an adult carve the face, hollowing out deep eyes with a potato peeler. Then, use a paring knife to carve the nose and mouth.
4. Roll the apple head in lemon juice and then roll it in salt.
5. Place the apple head on a cooling or drying rack and place in a dry location for two weeks or until it shrinks.

CONCOCTION TIPS & IDEAS:
♦ Use markers to add color to the lips, eyes and cheeks of your Little Apple Heads.
♦ Use yarn to create hair for your apple heads.

CANDY CLAY

Not only can you sculpt with this awesome clay, you can eat it!

WHAT YOU WILL NEED:

1 pound powdered sugar
1/3 cup corn syrup
1/2 tsp. salt
1/3 cup margarine (softened)
1 tsp. vanilla extract
5-7 drops food coloring

HOW TO CONCOCT IT:

1. Mix all ingredients together in a small bowl until blended. If the mixture is too sticky, add more powdered sugar.
2. Sculpt with your Candy Clay to create different animals, pretend fruits, and other sculptures you can eat!

CONCOCTION TIPS & IDEAS:

♦ Experiment by using different colors and different flavors of extract (banana, almond, etc.).
♦ Use Candy Clay sculptures to decorate the top of your favorite dessert.

SUPER SPRAY PAINT

This homemade spray paint is great for painting cool pictures, large signs and banners.

WHAT YOU WILL NEED:

1 Tbs. powder tempera paint
1 cup water
Spray bottle

HOW TO CONCOCT IT:

1. Mix paint and water together in a small bowl.
2. Pour the mixture into a spray bottle and paint.
3. Shake the Super Spray Paint bottle before each use.

CONCOCTION TIPS & IDEAS:

♦ Add 1 Tbs. of white school glue to your Super Spray Paint to make it shiny.

WACKY SPACE BALLS

These wild and Wacky Space Balls make great ornaments and look cool when hung from the ceiling.

WHAT YOU WILL NEED:

1/3 cup quick-setting Plaster of Paris
3 Tbs. water
1 Tbs. powder or liquid tempera paint
String or yarn
Balloon

HOW TO CONCOCT IT:

1. Blow up balloon.
2. Mix plaster, water, and paint together in a small bowl.
3. Soak string or yarn in the plaster mixture.
4. Squeeze excess plaster off the string or yarn and wrap it around the balloon. Then, sprinkle it with glitter.
5. Let the plaster dry for 2 hours and then pop the balloon with a pin.
6. Tie a string around the Wacky Space Ball and hang it as an ornament or from the ceiling.

CONCOCTION TIPS & IDEAS:

◆ Try adding liquid tempera paint to the plaster before dipping the yarn or string.
◆ Jazz up your Wacky Space Ball by painting it with liquid tempera paint.

CRAZY PRETZELS

Create soft, tasty pretzels in different crazy shapes and sizes.

WHAT YOU WILL NEED:

1 package yeast
1 Tbs. sugar
1 1/2 cups warm water
4 cups flour
1 tsp. salt
1 egg, beaten

HOW TO CONCOCT IT:

1. Mix water and yeast together in a large bowl until the yeast dissolves.
2. Add salt, sugar, and flour.
3. Mix and knead the dough until it is smooth.
4. Roll and twist the dough into letters, numbers, and animal shapes.
5. Lay the pretzels on a greased cookie sheet, brush with a beaten egg, then lightly sprinkle with extra salt.
6. Bake at 425 degrees for 12 to 15 minutes.

CONCOCTION TIPS & IDEAS:

♦ Add a few drops of food coloring to the Crazy Pretzel dough to create rainbow colored pretzels.

FLOWER PEOPLE

Surprise and delight unsuspecting visitors with flowers that look like people.

WHAT YOU WILL NEED:

White glue
Google eyes
Pipe cleaners
Flowers (sunflowers and large daisies work best)

HOW TO CONCOCT IT:

1. Using the white glue make two dots on the face of the flower.
2. Stick two google eyes onto the glue dots.
3. Bend a pipe cleaner into the shape of a mouth. Apply glue to the back of the pipe cleaner, then stick it onto the flower.

CONCOCTION TIPS & IDEAS:

♦ Bend green pipe cleaners around the flower stem to create arms and hands.
♦ Experiment by gluing a mouth and eyes on other types of plants besides flowers.

SHAKE & MAKE BUTTER

Have a blast creating tasty butter in minutes by shaking a zip bag full of kitchen ingredients.

WHAT YOU WILL NEED:

1 large zip bag or plastic container with lid
1 pint heavy whipping cream
1 pinch of salt

HOW TO CONCOCT IT:

1. Pour heavy whipping cream and salt into the large zip bag or container.
2. Seal the zip bag or container.
3. After 15 minutes of shaking the zip bag, chunks of butter will start to form.
4. Drain excess liquid from the zip bag or container, then seal it.
5. Store the butter in the refrigerator until you are ready to use it.

CONCOCTION TIPS & IDEAS:

♦ Push Shake & Make Butter chunks into a candy mold, place it in the refrigerator and pop out when hard.
♦ Add 1 Tbs. of honey or maple syrup to add more flavor to your Shake & Make Butter.

3-D POPCORN PAINT

Use 3-D Popcorn Paint just like you would use paint or crayons to color your favorite pictures.

WHAT YOU WILL NEED:

1 cup popped popcorn
2 Tbs. water
5-7 drops food coloring
Large plastic zip bag
White school glue

HOW TO CONCOCT IT:

1. Pour popcorn into a large zip bag.
2. Mix food coloring and water together and then pour the mixture on top of the popcorn.
3. Seal the zip bag and shake it until the popcorn changes color.
4. Pour the popcorn out on a paper towel to dry.
5. Use popcorn paint by filling the area you want to color with school glue and then cover the glue with the popcorn paint. Let the picture dry for 24 hrs. before moving or hanging it.

CONCOCTION TIPS & IDEAS:

♦ Use 3-D Popcorn Paint to create unique greeting cards and decorate gift boxes.
♦ Make interesting ornaments and mobiles by cutting shapes out of cardboard and covering them with 3-D Popcorn Paint. Hang your ornament or mobile up by poking a hole through it and then tying a piece of string or yarn through the hole.

GOOFY GLASS PAINT

This project works just like expensive store bought glass paints.

WHAT YOU WILL NEED:

1/4 cup white school glue
1/4 cup liquid tempera paint

HOW TO CONCOCT IT:

1. Mix glue and tempera paint together in a small bowl.
2. Use a paint brush to apply Goofy Glass Paint to the surface you wish to paint.
3. Let painted items dry overnight before using.

CONCOCTION TIPS & IDEAS:

♦ Give new life to old vases and jars by painting them with Goofy Glass Paint.
♦ Remove the label from and old peanut butter jar and paint it with Goofy Glass Paint to create a really cool pencil and pen holder.

INDIAN CORN JEWELRY

Indian Corn Jewelry has the look and feel of high polished stone jewelry.

WHAT YOU WILL NEED:

1/2 cup Indian corn kernels
Sewing needle
Thread
Small bowl
Water

HOW TO CONCOCT IT:

1. Pour corn kernels into a small bowl of water.
2. Let the corn kernels soak overnight or until soft.
3. Thread the needle, tying a knot at the end of the thread.
4. Have an adult push the needle through each soft kernel of corn until the necklace or bracelet is as long as you want it to be. Tie both ends of the thread together.

CONCOCTION TIPS & IDEAS:

♦ Glue dried corn kernels on a headband, hair comb, or hair clip to create matching accessories for your Indian Corn Jewelry.

COOL CRAYON TEE SHIRTS

Create some of the coolest tee shirts you have ever seen with nothing more than a box of crayons.

WHAT YOU WILL NEED:

Box of crayons
100% cotton tee shirt
Wax paper
Iron

HOW TO CONCOCT IT:

1. Using the box of crayons, create and color a picture or design on your cotton tee shirt.
2. Put the shirt on an ironing board.
3. Place a sheet of wax paper over the picture or design.
4. Place an iron on the cotton setting and have an adult iron the back of the wax paper for 15-30 seconds. This will make your design permanent.

CONCOCTION TIPS & IDEAS:

◆ Try making some Cool Crayon napkins, aprons, and place mats. Always make sure you only use 100% cotton fabric.
◆ Cool Crayon Tee Shirts are great for creating custom shirts for school clubs, scouts, or your next family reunion.

MAGIC PAINT

Your friends will be amazed when you send them an invisible message using Magic Paint.

WHAT YOU WILL NEED:

1 Tbs. baking soda
2 Tbs. water
4-6 drops food coloring
Paintbrush
Paper

HOW TO CONCOCT IT:

1. Mix 1 Tbs. water and 1 Tbs. baking soda together.
2. Dip your paintbrush into the baking soda water mixture and then write your mystery message on a sheet of paper.
3. Let the message completely dry.
4. To reveal your Magic Paint message mix together the remaining 1 Tbs. water and 4-6 drops of food coloring.
5. Using a brush, paint the water and food coloring mixture over the Magic Paint message. Your message will be revealed.

CONCOCTION TIPS & IDEAS:

♦ Try making a Magic Paint greeting card for a birthday or any other special occasion.
♦ Paint a Magic Paint picture to give to a friend or family member.

SURPRISE CHALK

With this concoction you can create sidewalk chalk with a secret surprise inside.

WHAT YOU WILL NEED:

1/3 cup quick-setting Plaster of Paris
1 Tbs. tempera paint
3 Tbs. water
Toilet paper tube
Coins, small rubber animals, or toy treasures

HOW TO CONCOCT IT:

1. Mix plaster, powdered tempera paint, and water together in a small bowl until blended.
2. Quickly spoon half of the mixture into a toilet paper tube sealed at one end with duct tape.
3. Place your surprise treasure in the toilet paper tube half full of the chalk mixture.
4. Spoon the remaining chalk mixture into the toilet paper tube.
5. Let the chalk dry 30-45 minutes.
6. Carefully peel the toilet paper tube away from the stick of chalk.

CONCOCTION TIPS & IDEAS:

◆ Create Sidewalk Chalk in different shapes by using plastic candy and soap molds.
◆ Make your Surprise Chalk sparkle by stirring 1 tsp. of glitter into the plaster mixture.

KOOKY CLINGERS

Create your very own Kooky Clingers for holidays. special occasions, or just for fun.

WHAT YOU WILL NEED:

1/4 cup white glue
7-10 drops food coloring
Plastic overhead sheet
Paint brush

HOW TO CONCOCT IT:

1. Mix white glue and food coloring together in a small
   bowl.
2. Brush a thick layer of the glue and food coloring mixture onto the plastic overhead sheet to create a design. Do
   not leave any blank spots or white spaces in your design.
3. Let the design set 24 hours or until dry.
4. Peel the design off the overhead sheet and stick to any glass surface.

CONCOCTION TIPS & IDEAS:

◆ Draw a picture on a sheet of paper, then lay the plastic overhead sheet on top of the paper. Trace the design
   with the food coloring and glue mixture to create fool proof stickers every time.
◆ Add a little bit of glitter to the glue mixture to make your Kooky Clingers sparkle.

FILTER FLOWERS

Create a bright colored bouquet of tye-dye flowers, using only a few household ingredients.

WHAT YOU WILL NEED:

3 cone shaped coffee filters
10-12 drops food coloring
1/4 cup water
Green pipe cleaner

HOW TO CONCOCT IT:

1. Mix water and food coloring together in a small dish. Repeat this step 2-3 times, using different colors of food coloring.
2. Fold each of the 3 coffee filters into fourths.
3. Dip each edge and corner of the filters in a different color of the food coloring water mixture.
4. Unfold the filters and set them on a paper towel until they are dry.
5. Place the 3 filters inside each other.
6. Grab the bottom point of the filters and twist the top 3 inches of the green pipe cleaner around the point. Pull the rest of the pipe cleaner straight down to form a stem.

CONCOCTION TIPS & IDEAS:

♦ Make a Filter Butterfly by clipping the points of two colored coffee filters in the middle of a clothes pin. Glue on google eyes and small pieces of black pipe cleaners for antennas.

CHOCOLATE BOWL

This tasty chocolate bowl makes the perfect dessert when served full of ice cream or fresh fruit.

WHAT YOU WILL NEED:

1 small balloon
1 cup semi-sweet chocolate chips

HOW TO CONCOCT IT:

1. Pour chocolate chips in a microwave bowl and place in the microwave for 5 minutes on the Medium setting. Remove from microwave and stir.
2. Keep repeating the above process until the chocolate chips are melted.
3. Blow up and tie the balloon, then dip it half way into the melted chocolate.
4. Let the balloon cool 3-4 minutes and then redip it in the melted chocolate.
5. Repeat step 4 until a thick layer of chocolate covers the balloon.
6. Let the chocolate cool for one hour and then pop the balloon using a pin.

CONCOCTION TIPS & IDEAS:

◆ Fill your chocolate bowl with pudding, ice cream, fresh fruit or your favorite dessert.

FLOWERS FOREVER

Dry and preserve fresh-cut flowers that will last for many years to come.

WHAT YOU WILL NEED:

1 cup Borax laundry booster
2 cups cornmeal
Cardboard shoe box
Fresh flowers

HOW TO CONCOCT IT:

1. Mix Borax and cornmeal together.
2. Cover the bottom of the shoe box with 3/4 inch of the Borax cornmeal mixture.
3. Cut the stems off the flowers and then place the flowers face down into the mixture as flat as possible.
4. Pour the remaining mixture on top of the flowers until they are completely covered.
5. Place the lid on top of the shoe box and set it in a dry place at room temperature for 3-4 weeks.
6. Remove dried flowers from the shoe box.

CONCOCTION TIPS & IDEAS:

◆ Flowers that have great drying results include: daisies, pansies, apple blossoms, asters, and violets.

FRUITY FINGER PAINTS

With this quick and easy concoction, you can make fruity scented commercial-quality finger paints.

WHAT YOU WILL NEED:

2 cups flour
2 Tbs. (2 envelopes) unsweetened drink mix
1/2 cup salt
3 cups hot water
3 Tbs. cooking oil
Freezer paper (Paint on the shiny side.)

HOW TO CONCOCT IT:

1. Mix flour, drink mix, and salt together.
2. Stir in water and cooking oil.
3. Paint on the shiny side of the freezer paper.

CONCOCTION TIPS & IDEAS:

♦ Challenge a friend or family member to a game of Fruity Finger Paint Hangman or Tic-Tac-Toe!
♦ Use a brush to paint with Fruity Finger Paints just as you would any other paint.

LIVING WORDS

Plant seeds and they grow into words and pictures that will amaze your friends and family.

WHAT YOU WILL NEED:

Grass seed
Potting soil
3-4 inch deep dish
Plant mister
Pencil

HOW TO CONCOCT IT:

1. Fill the dish with 2-3 inchs of potting soil.
2. Moisten the soil with a plant mister.
3. Use a pencil or stick to write words or draw a picture in the soil. This will create little trenches to plant the seeds in.
4. Carefully sprinkle grass seed into trenches made with the pencil.
5. Gently cover the seeds with a thin layer of soil and moisten with the plant mister.
6. Place your dish in an area where it will receive plenty of sunlight.
7. Lightly moisten the soil 1-2 times a day with the plant mister. Your Living Words will begin to sprout in 7-10 days.

CONCOCTION TIPS & IDEAS:

♦ Use chive seeds instead of grass seed to create living words.
♦ Try planting living words outside in the garden.

EDIBLE OCEAN

This tasty treat is great for birthday parties and is sure to amaze kids of all ages.

WHAT YOU WILL NEED:

4 cups pre-made blueberry flavored gelatin
4 clear plastic cups
Gummy fish

HOW TO CONCOCT IT:

1. Fill each cup with blueberry flavored gelatin.
2. Gently place 1-2 gummy fish into each cup.
3. Top with whipping cream and serve.

CONCOCTION TIPS & IDEAS:

♦ Fill a clear plastic party bag with blueberry flavored gelatin, place an orange gummy fish in the center of the gelatin and tie the bag shut with a ribbon. This project looks just like the gold fish in a bag many of us have won at the carnival or fair.

♦ Make a large Edible Ocean by filling a new fish bowl full of blueberry gelatin and gummy fish. You can even use grapes for gravel and shoe string licorice for seaweed.

COFFEE DOUGH

This concoction dries to an antique stone-like finish and is great for making small sculptures.

WHAT YOU WILL NEED:

1 cup coffee grounds
1 cup flour
1 cup salt
1 cup water

HOW TO CONCOCT IT:

1. Mix coffee grounds, flour, and salt together in a small bowl.
2. Add water and stir until the mixture turns into the consistency of a stiff clay.
3. If the clay is too sticky, knead in more flour.
4. Let Coffee Dough sculptures air dry or bake them in the oven at 200 degrees for 45 minutes. Larger sculptures may take longer to dry.

CONCOCTION TIPS & IDEAS:

◆ Make Coffee Dough beads to create a necklace or bracelet that will dry to a stone-like finish.

SQUEEZE CHALK

3-D Squeeze Chalk looks and feels like real chalk and dries in a matter of minutes.

WHAT YOU WILL NEED:

1/2 cup cornstarch
2 Tbs flour
1/4 cup water
4-6 drops of food coloring
medium zip bag

HOW TO CONCOCT IT:

1. Mix cornstarch and flour together in a small bowl.
2. Add water and 4-6 drops of food coloring.
3. Mix until the consistency of a thick paste. If paste is too dry, sprinkle with a little water and stir.
4. Pour the mixture into the zip bag and seal.
5. Cut a small hole in the corner of the zip bag and squeeze the chalk out of the bag and on the sidewalk.

CONCOCTION TIPS & IDEAS:

♦ Put 3-D Squeeze Chalk in a disposable cake decorating bag and use different tips to create unique designs.
♦ Add 1 tsp. of glitter to make your 3-D Squeeze Chalk sparkle.

CHOCOLATE SPOONS

Chocolate Spoons are great for eating ice cream and stirring hot cocoa.

WHAT YOU WILL NEED:

1 cup milk chocolate chips
12 plastic spoons
Wax paper

HOW TO CONCOCT IT:

1. Pour chocolate chips in a microwave bowl and place in the microwave for 5 minutes on the Medium setting, remove from microwave and stir.
2. Keep repeating the above process until the chocolate chips are melted.
3. Dip the end of the plastic spoons into the melted chocolate and place them on a sheet of wax paper to harden.

CONCOCTION TIPS & IDEAS:

♦ Try rolling your Chocolate Spoons in nuts and sprinkles before they harden.
♦ Turn your Chocolate Spoons into tasty gifts by wrapping the chocolate covered end of the spoon in plastic wrap and tying it with a ribbon.

CRYSTAL PAINT

This amazing paint actually crystallizes as it dries.

WHAT YOU WILL NEED:

1/8 cup liquid starch
1/8 cup water
4-6 drops food coloring

HOW TO CONCOCT IT:

1. Mix liquid starch and water together in a small bowl.
2. Stir in food coloring.
3. Use a brush to apply Crystal Paint to paper.

CONCOCTION TIPS & IDEAS:

♦ Use Crystal Paint to create unique holiday greeting cards, banners, and wrapping paper.

FRUITY LEATHER ROLL-UPS

Everyone will enjoy making our updated version of this delicious classic treat.

WHAT YOU WILL NEED:

2 cups applesauce
1/4 cup honey
Microwave safe plastic wrap
Microwave safe tray

HOW TO CONCOCT IT:

1. Stir applesauce and honey together in a small bowl.
2. Line a microwave safe tray with plastic wrap.
3. Pour a 1/8" layer of the applesauce honey mixture on top of the plastic wrap.
4. Dry the mixture in the microwave on the Medium setting for 3 minutes. Let the mixture cool for 3 minutes and then repeat the process until the fruity leather begins to dry. Results may vary depending on the wattage of the microwave.
5. Remove the fruity leather from the tray, keeping the plastic wrap as backing. Cut the leather into strips and roll it up.

CONCOCTION TIPS & IDEAS:

◆ For added flavor, sprinkle the applesauce honey mixture with cinnamon before placing it in the microwave.

SALTY PAINT

This concoction lets you turn regular table salt into beautiful, sparkling works of art.

WHAT YOU WILL NEED:

2 Tbs. table salt
1/2 Tbs. powder tempera paint
White school glue
Zip bag

HOW TO CONCOCT IT:

1. Pour salt and tempera paint into the zip bag and shake.
2. Repeat the above process to create Salty Paint in different colors.
3. Draw a picture on a sheet of paper using the white school glue.
4. Sprinkle the Salty Paint on top on of the glue, then carefully shake off any excess salt.
5. Let the Salty Paint dry overnight before you touch it.

CONCOCTION TIPS & IDEAS:

◆ Pour different colored layers of Salty Paint in an old baby food jar to create faux sand art.
◆ Give your Salty Paint a little more pizzazz by mixing in 1 tsp. of glitter.

PAINTED CARNATIONS

Create beautiful Painted Carnations using household ingredients and a little bit of science.

WHAT YOU WILL NEED:

White carnations
6-8 drops food coloring

HOW TO CONCOCT IT:

1. Cut carnation stems at an angle 5 inches away from the flower.
2. Fill a glass or small vase with 3 inches of water and stir in 6-8 drops of food coloring.
3. Place each flower in a different color of water.
4. After 24 hours the tips of the flower petals will have a light tint of color. The longer the flowers are left in the colored water, the brighter the color will be.

CONCOCTION TIPS & IDEAS:

♦ Create a bouquet of brightly colored flowers to make a beautiful Painted Carnation centerpiece.

MILKY WAY PAINT

This cool Kid Concoction paint looks like a creamy pastel color when it dries.

WHAT YOU WILL NEED:

1/2 cup powder nonfat milk
1/2 cup water
6-8 drops food coloring

HOW TO CONCOCT IT:

1. Mix milk, water, and food coloring together in a small bowl.
2. Repeat the above step several times to create different colors of Milky Way Paint.
3. Milky Way Paint dries in 1-2 hours.
4. Do not store Milky Way Paint or let it set out longer than a few hours.

CONCOCTION TIPS & IDEAS:

♦ Milky Way Paint is super for painting pictures of sunsets, skies, oceans, and lakes.
♦ Milky Way Paint makes a great "first paint" for young children.

BIRD COOKIES

Our feathered friends chirp over these tasty cookie treats that are for the birds.

WHAT YOU WILL NEED:

1 cup softened unsalted butter
3 beaten eggs
3 1/2 cups flour
1 tsp. baking soda
Pinch of salt
Mixed birdseed

HOW TO CONCOCT IT:

1. Stir flour, baking soda, and salt together in a large bowl.
2. Add buttter and eggs. Mix until well blended.
3. Roll dough out on a floured surface and cut different shapes with cookie cutters.
4. Make a hole in the top of each cookie with a drinking straw.
5. Press birdseed into each side of the cookies.
6. Bake at 350 degrees for 10-12 minutes.
7. When Bird Cookies are cool, tie a ribbon or string through the hole and hang on a tree limb.

CONCOCTION TIPS & IDEAS:

♦ Make another great bird treat by covering a pine cone with peanut butter and rolling it in birdseed. Tie a string around the pine cone and hang it outside on a tree branch.

CONFETTI BALLOONS

This fun concoction is perfect for birthday parties, New Year's Eve, or any festive occasion.

WHAT YOU WILL NEED:

1 large balloon
1/4 cup paper confetti
Toothpick
Funnel

HOW TO CONCOCT IT:

1. Pull the balloon over the end of the funnel.
2. Pour the confetti into the balloon.
3. Remove the balloon from the funnel and blow it up while being careful not to get any confetti in your mouth.
4. Tie the balloon shut.
5. When you are ready to pop your Confetti Balloon, hold it away from your face and pop it with a toothpick.

CONCOCTION TIPS & IDEAS:

♦ Roll up a message written on a small piece of paper and place it inside of the balloon before you blow it up.
♦ Use felt tipped markers to decorate the outside of your Confetti Balloons.

FROSTED GLASS CANDLES

Create the look and feel of real frosted glass using salt and nail polish.

WHAT YOU WILL NEED:

Table salt
Assorted colors of non-flammable nail polish
Baby food jar

HOW TO CONCOCT IT:

1. Remove the label from the baby food jar.
2. Paint a design on the outside of the baby food jar using different colors of nail polish.
3. Sprinkle salt on top of the nail polish while it is still wet.
4. Let your finished candle holder dry overnight.
5. Place a small votive candle inside the baby food jar.

CONCOCTION TIPS & IDEAS:

◆ Use clear nail polish to create the look of white frosted glass.

KOOKIE COOKIE PAINT

With this wacky and wild concoction, young Picassos can actually eat their works of art.

WHAT YOU WILL NEED:

1 beaten egg yolk
4-6 drops food coloring
Store bought sugar cookie dough
Wax paper
Paintbrushes

HOW TO CONCOCT IT:

1. Mix the egg yolk and food coloring together in a small bowl.
   Repeat this process several times to create different colors of Kookie Cookie Paint.
2. Roll the cookie dough out on wax paper and cut with assorted shapes and sizes of cookie cutters.
3. Place the cookies on a greased cookie sheet.
4. Using your Kookie Cookie Paint and paintbrushes, you can create various different designs and pictures on your cookies.
5. Bake as directed on the package of cookie dough.

CONCOCTION TIPS & IDEAS:

♦ Before baking, sprinkle cookies with colored sugar or candy sprinkles.

CANDY JEWELRY

Create bright colored necklaces and bracelets you can wear and eat.

WHAT YOU WILL NEED:

Shoe string licorice
Cereal with holes in the middle
Hard candy with holes in the middle

HOW TO CONCOCT IT:

1. Cut a piece of shoe string licorice to the desired length. Longer for a necklace or shorter for a bracelet.
2. String cereal and hard candy onto the shoe string licorice, creating different designs and patterns.
3. Tie the loose ends of the licorice together around your neck or wrist.

CONCOCTION TIPS & IDEAS:

♦ Candy jewelry makes great birthday favors or a wonderful activity for a slumber party.

CRYSTAL SCULPTING

Create three-dimensional crystal sculptures that make dazzling tree ornaments and package ties.

WHAT YOU WILL NEED:

Large jar
Borax laundry booster
Pipe cleaners
Pencil
String
Water
Food coloring

HOW TO CONCOCT IT:

1. Have an adult fill the jar with boiling water.
2. Pour Borax into the jar one spoonful at a time until it no longer dissolves and settles on the bottom of the jar.
3. Stir in 10-12 drops of food coloring.
4. Bend a pipe cleaner into different shapes, sizes and forms.
5. Tie one end of the string around the pipe cleaner sculpture and the other around a pencil.
6. Place the pencil on the jar lid so the pipe cleaner is suspended in the middle of the Borax solution.
7. Let the solution stand overnight. Remove the crystal covered sculpture and let it dry.

CONCOCTION TIPS & IDEAS:

♦ Tie several different Crystal Sculptures together to create a mobile for your bedroom.

MAGIC PHOTO ART

Transform black and white photos from newspapers or magazines into wacky works of art!

WHAT YOU WILL NEED:

Black and white picture from a magazine or newspaper
Color pencils, markers, crayons or watercolor paints

HOW TO CONCOCT IT:

1. Cut a black and white picture from a magazine or newspaper.
2. Give the picture new life by coloring it in with color pencils, markers, crayons, or watercolor paints.

CONCOCTION TIPS & IDEAS:

♦ Take a picture of your family, friends, or pet and copy it on a black & white photocopier, then color it in.
♦ Try creating your own greeting cards with your magic photos.

DRYER LINT CLAY

This velvet-like dough is a great way to recycle old dryer lint.

WHAT YOU WILL NEED:

3 cups dryer lint
2 cups warm water
2/3 cup wheat flour

HOW TO CONCOCT IT:

1. Mix all ingredients togehter in a large sauce pan.
2. Have an adult cook the mixture over low heat, stirring constantly until the mixture starts to hold together.
3. Pour the mixture out onto several layers of newspapers to cool.
4. Dryer Lint Clay dries to a hard, smooth finish.

CONCOCTION TIPS & IDEAS:

♦ Shape the Dryer Lint Clay over bottles, boxes, and balloons.

APPLE CANDLE HOLDERS

This old-fashioned concoction is the perfect way to turn fresh fruit into elegant candle holders.

WHAT YOU WILL NEED:

Apple
Apple corer
1 cup lemon juice
Candle

HOW TO CONCOCT IT:

1. Use the apple corer to remove the core from the apple.
2. Soak the apple in lemon juice for 2 minutes.
3. Insert the candle into the cored apple.

CONCOCTION TIPS & IDEAS:

♦ Use different colors of apples to create your Apple Candle Holders.
♦ Push cloves into the outside of the apple to create different designs.

SHAKE & MAKE WHIPPED CREAM

Use a peanut butter jar and a few kitchen ingredients to create tasty whipped cream in minutes.

WHAT YOU WILL NEED:

1 large plastic peanut butter jar
1 pint heavy whipping cream
1 tsp. vanilla extract
2 Tbs. powdered sugar

HOW TO CONCOCT IT:

1. Pour heavy whipping cream, powdered sugar and vanilla extract into a plastic peanut butter jar..
2. Screw the lid on the peanut butter jar as tightly as possible.
3. Shake the jar in an up-and-down motion for 5-10 minutes or until the mixture turns into a thick, fluffy cream.

CONCOCTION TIPS & IDEAS:

◆ Create different flavors of Shake & Make Whipped Cream by adding a tsp. of chocolate syrup, maple syrup, or flavored extracts.
◆ Add a drop of food coloring to the mixture before shaking to create whipping cream in an assortment of bright colors.

SMOKE EGGS

This fun and safe concoction is a great way for kids of all ages to celebrate Independence Day.

WHAT YOU WILL NEED:

Eggs
Baby powder
Tape
Felt tip markers

HOW TO CONCOCT IT:

1. Tap the narrow end of the egg with the back of a spoon to create a 1 inch opening.
2. Hold the egg upside down over a bowl and shake out the contents of the egg. Wash out the eggshell and your hands with warm soapy water.
3. Let the eggshell dry and then decorate the shell with felt tip markers.
4. Fill the eggshell with baby powder and then seal it with a piece of tape.
5. Throw the egg against the driveway or sidewalk to create a smoke cloud.
6. Clean up the mess left by the smoke eggs, using a broom and a garden hose or bucket of water.

CONCOCTION TIPS & IDEAS:

◆ Create Confetti Eggs for your next New Year's Eve celebration or birthday party by filling the eggshell with confetti instead of baby powder.

GREENHOUSE IN A BAG

This nifty concoction is a great way to see how seeds sprout and grow.

WHAT YOU WILL NEED:

Small plastic zip bag
3 wet cotton balls
2-3 large seeds (beans work best)
Clear tape

HOW TO CONCOCT IT:

1. Place the wet cotton balls in the zip bag with the seeds placed against them.
2. Seal the zip bag and tape it to a window where it will receive plenty of sunlight. Your seed should begin to sprout in 3-5 days.
3. After your sprouts grow at least 1 inch, you can transplant it in soil, so the plant may continue to grow.

CONCOCTION TIPS & IDEAS:

♦ Make several Greenhouses in a Bag, using different types of seeds. Observe the seeds to see which ones sprout first and how fast they grow.

CHOCOLATE CLAY

With this concoction, you can sculpt and eat your incredible clay creations.

WHAT YOU WILL NEED:

10 oz. semi-sweet chocolate chips
1/3 cup light corn syrup

HOW TO CONCOCT IT:

1. Pour chocolate chips into a microwave safe bowl and place in the microwave on High for 1 minute.
2. Stir the chocolate and place back in the microwave for 1 minute or until the chocolate is melted.
3. Stir in the corn syrup.
4. Spread the chocolate out 1/2" thick on a sheet of wax paper.
5. Let the chocolate set overnight. It will stiffen and become pliable. Now you are ready to sculpt!

CONCOCTION TIPS & IDEAS:

♦ Make Chocolate Clay in a wide variety of different colors by using white chocolate chips and stirring in a few drops of food coloring before the corn syrup is added.

TOOTHPASTE PUTTY

With Toothpaste Putty you can have fun creating beads and colorful sculptures that dry hard as a rock.

WHAT YOU WILL NEED:

1 Tbs. white school glue
2 Tbs. cornstarch
1/2 Tbs. water
1/2 Tbs toothpaste
1-2 drops food coloring

HOW TO CONCOCT IT:

1. Mix glue, cornstarch, food coloring and toothpaste together in a small bowl.
2. Add water and stir until the mixture turns into a clump of putty.
3. Toothpaste Putty must be used very quickly. It will begin to harden in 25 minutes or less and will be completely dry in 24 hours.

CONCOCTION TIPS & IDEAS:

♦ Push Toothpaste Putty into candy molds to create sculptures in a wide variety of shapes and sizes.

FUNNY FACE TOAST

With this concoction you can create funny faces, pictures and designs that will brighten up your morning toast.

WHAT YOU WILL NEED:

2 Tbs. milk
2 drops food coloring
Paintbrush
Slice of bread

HOW TO CONCOCT IT:

1. Mix milk and food coloring together in a small dish.
2. Use a paintbrush to paint a face or design on the slice of bread.
3. Toast the bread in a toaster set on the light setting.

CONCOCTION TIPS & IDEAS:

♦ Funny Face Toast is great when used to make peanut butter and jelly or BLT sandwiches.
♦ Use Funny Face toast to kick off a holiday breakfast. Paint a heart on your toast for Valentine's Day, a shamrock for St. Patrick's Day, a pumpkin for Halloween, etc.

BEAN MOSAICS

Create festive and colorful mosaic pictures using dried beans and a little imagination.

WHAT YOU WILL NEED:

White glue
Dried beans (lima, pinto, black, kidney, etc.)
Heavy paper or cardboard
Pencil

HOW TO CONCOCT IT:

1. Use a pencil and draw a picture on a heavy sheet of paper or cardboard.
2. Use white glue to fill in a small area of the picture.
3. Immediately cover the school glue with the beans. Repeat the process until the entire picture is completed.

CONCOCTION TIPS & IDEAS:

♦ Use Bean Mosaics to decorate the front of greeting cards, picture frames, and small boxes.
♦ Light color beans can be stained by painting them with the following mixture: 1 Tbs. water and 3-4 drops food coloring.

RUBBER BAND BALL

This goofy concoction bounces in crazy patterns and will keep you guessing what it will do next.

WHAT YOU WILL NEED:

Tennis ball
Bag of multi-color rubber bands

HOW TO CONCOCT IT:

1. Wrap the tennis ball with a layer of rubber bands.
2. Continue wrapping the tennis ball with rubber bands until you can no longer see the original color of the ball.
3. The more rubber bands you add to the ball, the larger it will become.

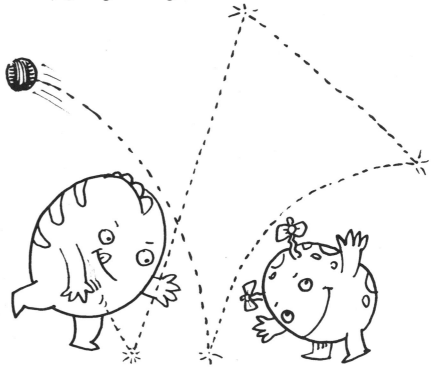

CONCOCTION TIPS & IDEAS:

♦ Have a contest with your friends or school classmates to see who can create the largest Rubber Band Ball!
♦ Make a Rubber Band Ball as a gift for a teacher, office worker, or anyone who uses rubber bands.

WHIPPED CREAM FINGER PAINT

This delicious finger paint is a fun way to introduce small children to finger painting.

WHAT YOU WILL NEED:

1/4 cup whipped cream
2-4 drops food coloring
Freezer paper

HOW TO CONCOCT IT:

1. Mix whipped cream and food coloring together in a small bowl. Repeat this step to create various different colors of Whipped Cream Paint.
2. Finger paint on the shiny side of the freezer paper, it works just as well as store bought finger painting paper and it's a lot less expensive.

CONCOCTION TIPS & IDEAS:

♦ Add a drop of vanilla, peppermint, or banana extract to give Whipped Cream Finger Paint a wonderful scent and a great taste.

CREPE PAPER DOUGH

This fun concoction is a creative way to recycle crepe paper after a party or celebration.

WHAT YOU WILL NEED:

1 roll crepe paper
1/2 cup flour
1/4 cup salt
Large bowl of water

HOW TO CONCOCT IT:

1. Tear the roll of crepe paper into small pieces and soak it in the large bowl of water overnight until it turns into pulp.
2. Drain the water off the pulp.
3. Measure one packed cup of pulp into a bowl.
4. Mix in flour and salt.
5. Knead the mixture with your hand until it turns into a dough. If the dough is too sticky, add more flour.

CONCOCTION TIPS & IDEAS:

- ◆ Use Crepe Paper Dough to create beautiful tie-dye like beads for bracelets and necklaces.
- ◆ Mold Crepe Paper Dough around a small tin can to create a beautiful vase for fresh flowers.

FROSTING DOUGH

This edible dough is a fantastic way to top off any birthday cake or cupcake.

WHAT YOU WILL NEED:

1 can frosting
1 1/2 cups powdered sugar
1 cup peanut butter
6-8 drops food coloring

HOW TO CONCOCT IT:

1. Mix frosting, powdered sugar, food coloring and peanut butter together in a large bowl.
2. Knead the mixture until it turns into a dough.
3. Mold with Frosting Dough as you would any other dough.

CONCOCTION TIPS & IDEAS:

♦ Use Frosting Dough to create animals, people, flowers, and other unique works of edible art.
♦ Frosting Dough sculptures can be used to garnish desserts such as cake, pies, and ice cream.

SPAGHETTI ART

Turn cold leftover spaghetti into the hottest works of 3-D art you've ever seen.

WHAT YOU WILL NEED:

White school glue
Cold cooked spaghetti
Wax paper
Assorted colors of glitter

HOW TO CONCOCT IT:

1. Pour some school glue into a small bowl.
2. Dip a few strands of spaghetti at a time into the white school glue.
3. Create different designs by arranging the glue covered spaghetti strands on a sheet of wax paper. Make sure all the strands of spaghetti are connected and touching each other.
4. Sprinkle the glue covered spaghetti with glitter.
5. Let your design set overnight or until dry.
6. Carefully peel the wax paper away from the Spaghetti Art.

CONCOCTION TIPS & IDEAS:

♦ Use Spaghetti Art and some string to create awesome mobiles, ornaments, and package ties.
♦ Create cool winter window decorations by creating spaghetti snowflakes and sprinkling with silver glitter.

CRAYON MELT ART

You'll be amazed as you watch old crayons melt together to create stained glass like designs.

WHAT YOU WILL NEED:

Old crayons
Wax paper
Kitchen grater
Iron

HOW TO CONCOCT IT:

1. Have an adult grate up the old crayons and separate them by color.
2. Use a felt tip pen to draw a bold design on a sheet of wax paper.
3. Fill the design with the grated bits of crayons.
4. Carefully place another sheet of wax paper on top of your crayon filled drawing.
5. Have an adult iron the top of the wax paper with an iron on the low setting. Continue ironing until the crayon wax melts together.

CONCOCTION TIPS & IDEAS:

♦ Use Crayon Melt Art to create sparkling sun catchers and other stained glass like window decorations.

BLAST BALL

This original Kid Concoctions creation will provide hours of exciting outdoor fun.

WHAT YOU WILL NEED:

12 inch balloon
Woman's nylon stocking leg or knee high stocking
Water

HOW TO CONCOCT IT:

1. Place the balloon inside the nylon.
2. Put the balloon over the end of a water faucet and fill with approximately 3 Tbs. of water.
3. Blow up the balloon with air until it is 6-8 inches in diameter. Tie the balloon shut.
4. Carefully push the balloon down into the toe area of the nylon.
5. Tie a knot in the nylon just below the balloon, leaving a long tail.

CONCOCTION TIPS & IDEAS:

♦ Play with your blast ball in a grassy area, keeping it away from sharp objects.
♦ Grab the Blast Ball by the tail and swing it through the air.

PEPPERMINT WREATHS

Peppermint wreaths are a great alternative to hanging candy canes on the Christmas Tree.

WHAT YOU WILL NEED:

Bag of peppermint discs
Small aluminum pie tins
Cookie sheet
Ribbon

HOW TO CONCOCT IT:

1. Arrange peppermint discs in pie tins, in the shape of a circle, making sure the discs are touching each other. Place on cookie sheet.
2. Place the cookie sheet in a pre-heated oven at 250 degrees for 3-5 minutes or until the pepermint discs melt together.
3. Remove the cookie sheet from the oven and let the Peppermint Wreaths cool for 15 minutes.
4. Use a spatula to carefully remove the cooled Peppermint Wreaths from the pie tins.
5. Use ribbon to tie a bow around the top of the Peppermint Wreaths.

CONCOCTION TIPS & IDEAS:

♦ Use different types of hard candy and your imagination to create wreaths and other original designs.

SUPER SOAPY DOUGH

You'll have hours of fun creating, molding, and squeezing this great smelling dough.

WHAT YOU WILL NEED:

2 cups flour
1/2 cup salt
1 Tbs. liquid soap
Water

HOW TO CONCOCT IT:

1. Mix flour, salt, liquid soap, and food coloring together in a small bowl.
2. Slowly add water until a workable dough is formed. The amount of water will vary depending on the brand of liquid soap used.
3. If the dough becomes too sticky, add a little more flour.
4. Mold with Super Soapy Dough just as you would any other type of dough or clay.

CONCOCTION TIPS & IDEAS:

♦ Add a little color to your Super Soapy Dough by adding 4-6 drops of food coloring to the ingredients before mixing.

ICE LANTERNS

Light up a dark winter's night with these warm, inviting crystal Ice Lanterns.

WHAT YOU WILL NEED:

Large plastic bowl
Plastic yogurt container full of stones or coins

HOW TO CONCOCT IT:

1. Place 2 inches of water into the large plastic bowl and freeze.
2. Place the yogurt container full of stones or coins in the center of the frozen ice bowl.
3. Pour more water into the bowl until it almost reaches the rim of the yogurt container and freeze.
4. Run warm water over the outside of the plastic bowl and the ice bowl should pop out.
5. Remove the stones or coins from the yogurt container and pour in warm water. Remove the yogurt container when it becomes loose.
6. Have an adult put a small votive candle in the opening left by the yogurt container and place it outside.

CONCOCTION TIPS & IDEAS:

♦ Create Ice Lanterns in a wide variety of colors by mixing in a few drops of food coloring in with the water before freezing it.

POTATO DOUGH

We came up with this wacky dough while figuring out what to do with leftover mashed potatoes.

WHAT YOU WILL NEED:

2 cups mashed potatoes
1 1/2 cups flour
4-6 drops food coloring

HOW TO CONCOCT IT:

1. Mix mashed potatoes and flour together in a large bowl.
2. Add 4-6 drops of food coloring and stir until the color is evenly blended.
3. Use Potato Dough as you would any other type of dough. Do not store or reuse Potato Dough.

CONCOCTION TIPS & IDEAS

♦ Add a few drops of extract or 1 Tbs. of unsweetened drink mix to give Potato Dough a wide variety of different scents and colors. If using drink mix, omit food coloring from the concoction.

Index

Index